MY VERY FIRST

Colours
Shapes, Sizes,
and Opposites
Book

ANGELA WILKES

DORLING KINDERSLEY
LONDON • NEW YORK • STUTTGART

DK

A DORLING KINDERSLEY BOOK

First published in Great Britain in 1993
by Dorling Kindersley Limited,
9 Henrietta Street, London WC2E 8PS
Reprinted 1994, 1997

Copyright © 1993 Dorling Kindersley Limited, London

Visit us on the World Wide Web at
http://www.dk.com

Photography (p.6 ladybird & fish; front cover fish)
copyright © 1991 Jerry Young

A CIP catalogue record for this book is
available from the British Library

ISBN 0-7513-5100-8

Colour reproduction by Colourscan
Printed in Italy by L.E.G.O.

Contents

Note to parents and teachers

My Very First Colours, Shapes, Sizes, and Opposites Book is a bright and colourful picture book for you and your child to share. Packed with photographs of familiar objects, it is the ideal way to introduce young children to early learning concepts.

With so many pictures to look at and talk about, this book offers a wide range of learning opportunities. You can introduce concepts such as colours, shapes, sizes, and opposites and encourage your child to count, compare, and sort the different objects on the page and in the world around them. Each concept is introduced with everyday examples that children can identify and name. Interactive puzzles help to reinforce what has been learned and make the learning process fun.

You can also use this book to develop your child's reading skills. By pointing to each object as you read out the word label, you can encourage your child to associate the image with the written word – one of the very first steps in learning to read. An alphabetical index has been included so that children can use the book as a first picture dictionary.

Colours

Red

strawberries

daisy

ladybird

tomato

fire engine

Blue

butterfly

blueberries

jeans

fish

Yellow

canary

lemon

buttercups

bananas

Green

leaves

apple

limes

lizard

More colours

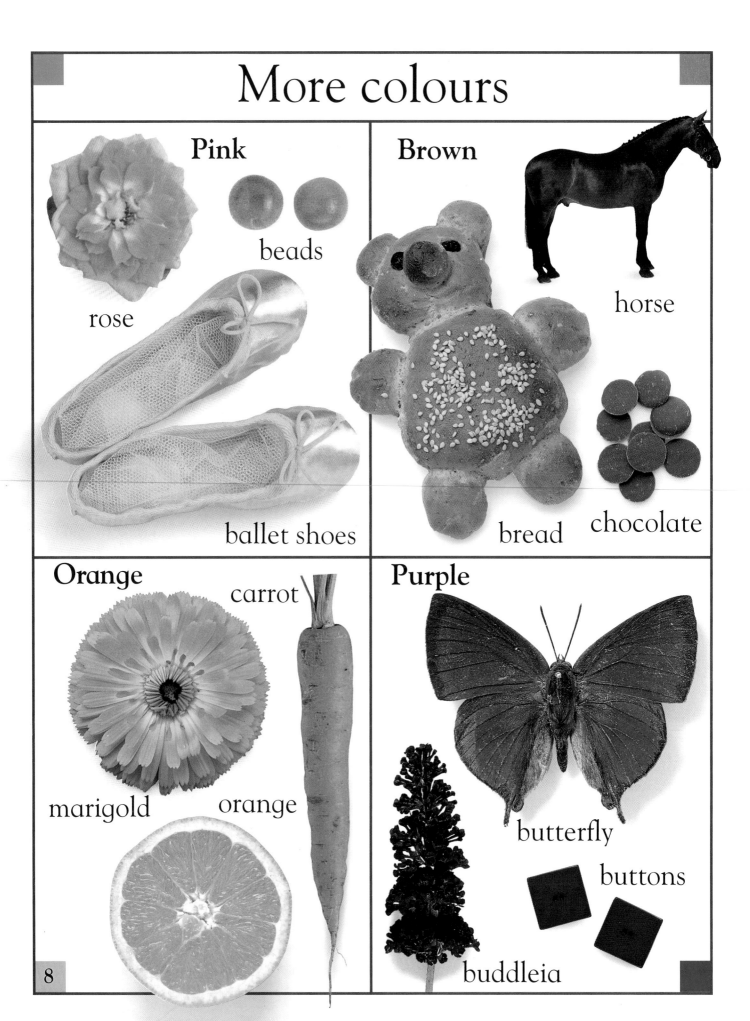

Pink

rose

beads

ballet shoes

Brown

horse

bread

chocolate

Orange

carrot

marigold

orange

Purple

butterfly

buttons

buddleia

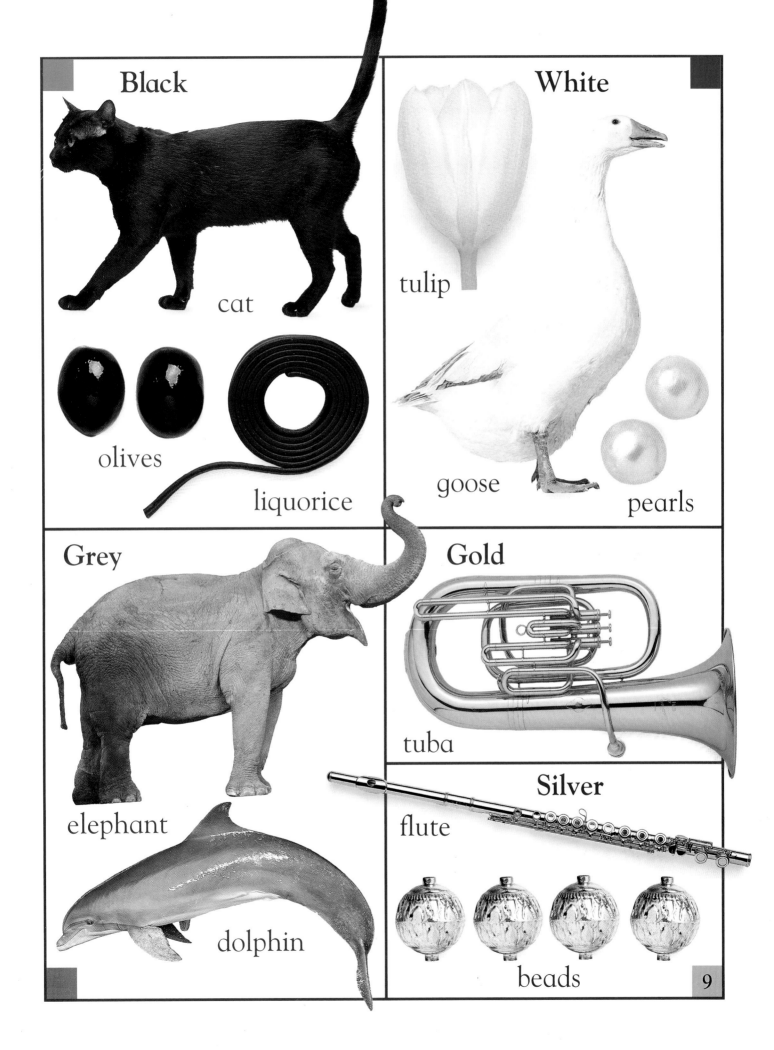

Black

cat

olives

liquorice

White

tulip

goose

pearls

Grey

elephant

dolphin

Gold

tuba

Silver

flute

beads

Colour puzzles

Flower wheel

How many
different colours
can you see?

How many red
roses can you
count?

How many yellow
roses can you count?

Can you count the
yellow daffodils?

Can you see
an orange lily?

10

More or less?

Are there more green
or red peppers?

Are there more red apples
or green apples?

Mix and match

Can you match each tractor to the right colour trailer?

Shapes

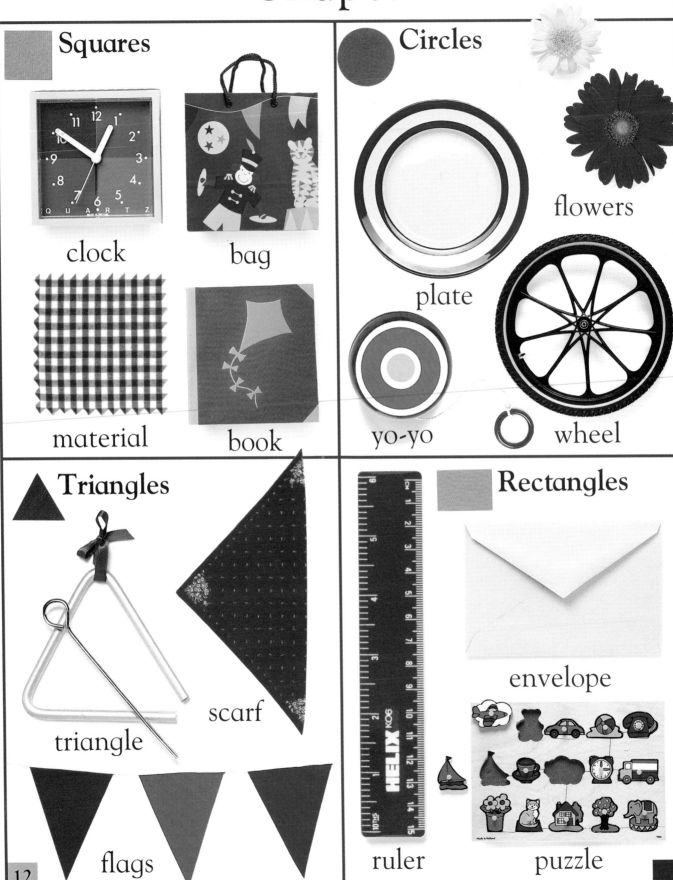

Squares

clock

bag

material

book

Circles

plate

yo-yo

wheel

flowers

Triangles

triangle

scarf

flags

Rectangles

envelope

ruler

puzzle

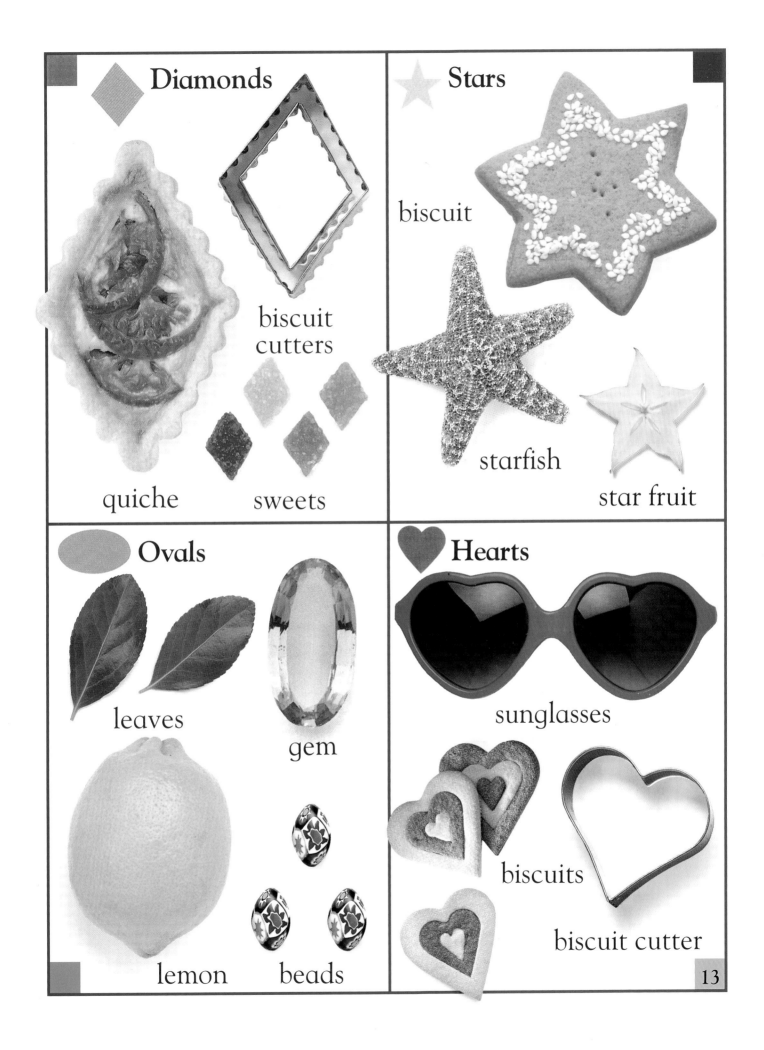

Diamonds

biscuit
cutters

quiche

sweets

Stars

biscuit

starfish

star fruit

Ovals

leaves

gem

lemon

beads

Hearts

sunglasses

biscuits

biscuit cutter

13

Solid shapes

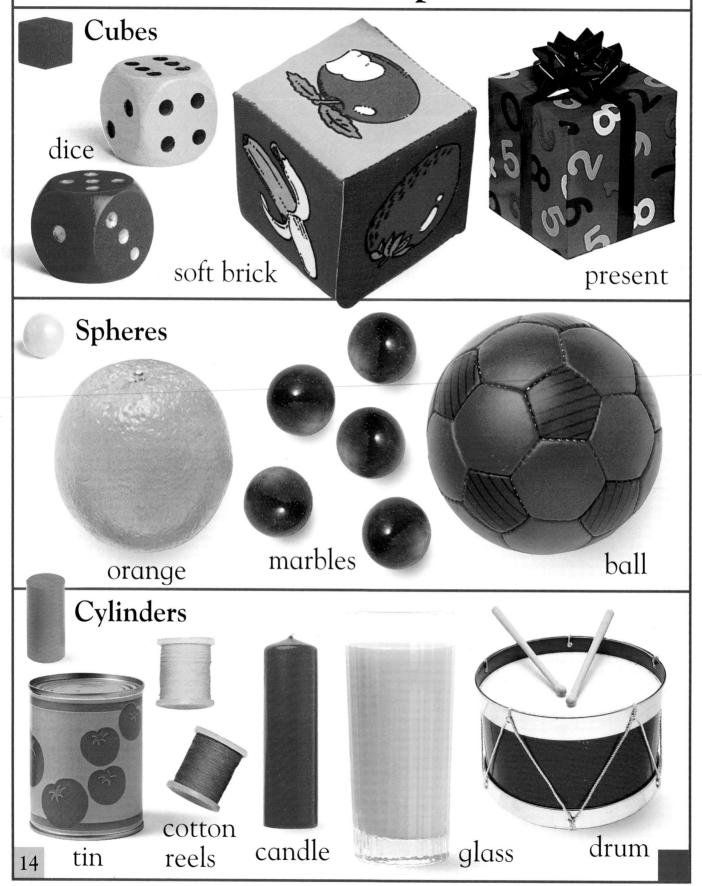

Cubes

dice

soft brick

present

Spheres

orange

marbles

ball

Cylinders

tin

cotton reels

candle

glass

drum

14

Cones

ice-cream

hat

Pyramids

boxes

Shape puzzle

How many different shapes can you count?

ball

candles

brick

wool

beakers

cake

rolling pin

Sizes

Big and small

cat

tiger

Big, bigger, biggest

tanker

SDF 304

fire engine

tractor

16

Small, smaller, smallest

five-
year-
old

three-
year-
old

one-
year-
old

Sorting sizes

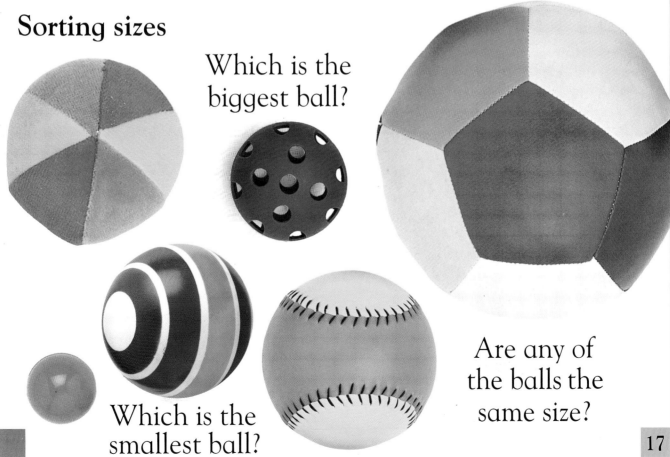

Which is the
biggest ball?

Which is the
smallest ball?

Are any of
the balls the
same size?

17

Opposites

big

small

thick

thin

long

short

soft

hard

down

up

front

back

open

closed

narrow

wide

left

right

happy

sad

19

Pairs and partners

These things come in pairs.

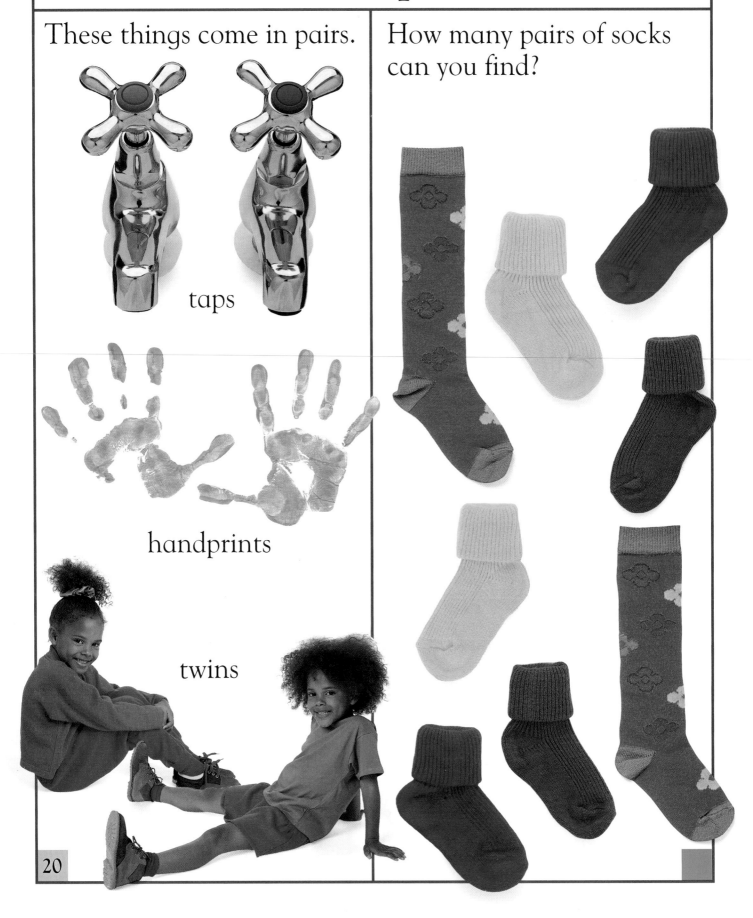

taps

handprints

twins

How many pairs of socks can you find?

These things belong together. They are called partners.

knife and fork

paint and paintbrush

hat and mittens

Can you match up the different partners?

pot

track

racquet

plant

toy train

ball

Index